BUILDING BRIDGES

10 STEPS TO ENGAGE YOUTH

Bevin Carpenter
with
Debra Tavaras

Foreword by Neil Shorthouse

Building Bridges Consulting LLC
Atlanta

Building Bridges: 10 Steps of Engagement
Copyright © 2018 Bevin Carpenter
All rights reserved. In accordance with the U.S. Copyright Act of 1976, the scanning, uploading, and electronic sharing of any part of this book without the permission of the publisher constitute unlawful piracy and theft of the author's intellectual property. If you would like to use material from the book (other than for review purposes), prior written permission must be obtained by contacting Bevin Carpenter using bevin.carpenter@icloud.com. Thank you for supporting the author's rights.

Building Bridges Consulting LLC
Atlanta, GA
bb2connect.com

Credits
Cover Design: Orin Carpenter
Interior Design: Laura Lis Scott
Graphic Artist: Justin Douglas
Editorial: Leslie Lapides, Stephanie Hines & Carla Dupont

ISBN: 978-0-692-19267-2

DEDICATION

*This book is dedicated to my parents,
Robert E. Carpenter (1942–2005, R.I.H.)
and mother Christine B. Carpenter.
I love you both for the examples you have been
and for the standard of excellence you held me to.
I love you and thank you.
~ Bevin Carpenter ~*

Acknowledgements

I would like to thank everyone who has been an influence in my life. I especially would like to thank Debra Tavaras for planting the seed of writing a book and staying on me until I did. I would like to thank my brother Orin Carpenter for his inspiration and sharing his gift by creating the artwork for the cover. Last but not least, I would like to thank my daughter Stephanie Hines, who serves as the reviser, and Tasha Tavaras for her marketing skills and all the advice throughout this journey. I am truly a blessed man and with your support I hope this book serves as an inspiration to others.

FOREWORD

"Building Bridges" is a small book destined to have a huge impact. Bevin Carpenter brings us face-to-face with disarming wisdom that creates a path to success with our nation's No. 1 resource: her children. Everyone aspiring to love, serve and lead kids: teachers, social workers, doctors, youth workers, counselors, advocates, colleges of education, clergy . . . moms and dads, too, will be challenged and energized by practicing all of Bevin's must-do common-sense lessons.
Neil Shorthouse
Co-founder
Communities In Schools

Contents

ACKNOWLEDGEMENTS v
FOREWORD vii

INTRODUCTION 1
THE JOURNEY 7
STEPS 11

    I. KNOW THEIR NAME 13
    II. LISTEN 23
    III. DON'T JUDGE 33
    IV. STAY IN YOUR LANE 41
    V. BE PERSONABLE 49
    VI. POSITIVE SPEECH 57
    VII. TONE 67
    VIII. RELEVANCE 73
    IX. BE CONSISTENT 81
    X. BE PATIENT 89

CLOSING 95

ABOUT THE AUTHOR 99
ABOUT THE ARTIST 101
QUOTES 103

BUILDING BRIDGES

INTRODUCTION

ENGAGING YOUTH IS A PASSION OF MINE. Because of all the one-sided media coverage about our youth and society's uneven portrayal of them in America, I feel charged to write this book. Our youth are to be celebrated for their contributions, not treated like zombies, with adults fearing them as though they are a different species. It is far more meaningful to engage and have a conversation with them.

The media stokes fear of being near our youth. That fear sets up paralysis, which keeps others from engaging with them. Only through conversation can you have empathy and an appreciation for someone else's life. I want us to travel together on this journey and look at each Step of Engagement from both a literal and figurative perspective. This journey will be done through the lens of my life, along with the lens of a few other people's lives.

Through my work with students, I have realized today's youth don't feel the comfort of community. Many have a great appreciation for family and even for an adult outside their home, but a connection to the community (or village) is missing. In this book, I will share with you my 10 Steps of Engagement. Hopefully, we can strengthen the village concept or revive it in new terms for our schools and youth.

Now let's start the journey of how to engage marginalized youth in America: land of the free, home of the brave.

A little about me . . .

I was born in Memphis, Tenn., in 1965, at the end of the Baby Boomer era and the start of the Gen X movement. Maybe this is why I can relate to those older than me (Baby Boomers) and those younger (Millennials) because I'm kind of a middle link. This is why I believe one of my gifts is the ability to connect people to their passion along with pointing them in the direction of resources that will help them achieve their greatness. This comes from watching parents who have lived their lives serving and helping others.

My mother and father graduated from Hamilton High School together. My father served in the U.S. Air Force, retired with an honorable discharge, married my mom, and I was born. I was not old enough to have experienced the separate restrooms, water fountains or "blacks only" days for public places like the zoo that allowed blacks to attend only one day a week. But, because I was born at the closing of that era, my parents made sure I knew my history. They spoke about their experiences to make it real for my younger brother and me.

I was born a few months after Malcolm X was assassinated and my brother was born a few months after Rev. Dr. Martin Luther King Jr. was assassinated. His assassination was a death blow to mankind and humanity in America. I was too young to know what all the commotion was about. After reading the history of that time, it resonated with me, learning about the tanks and soldiers in the streets, seeing sadness in adults' faces and the many tears that flowed. Of course, there is no way I could fully remember or understand why it happened, but there is a feeling of connection as I watch the videos of that time.

Through my maturity, I understand why and how I can make a difference. I am the child of educated parents who believed education would be the currency of the 21st century. Our home had plenty of books, stories of famous leaders and entertainers, education and business books, and even comics. My all-time favorite was the World Book Encyclopedia. As children, we had to learn how to entertain ourselves through imagination.

Many homes had one record player and one TV in the den. The TV only had four stations and never had anything a small kid like myself wanted to watch. As for the record player, my parents had a rule that you had to be "older" to touch it. So, growing up, children lived for going outside to play. Playing with friends or alone with my GI Joe, race track, skates, skateboard or cruising on a Big Wheel or bike was the highlight of my day.

We were forced to interact with each other because that was how society operated. My mother was a teacher and site director in Head Start (which I graduated from) before she became a kindergarten teacher with the Memphis City School

System, which she eventually retired from. Five of her siblings also retired from the education field. I graduated from kindergarten at the Centenary United Methodist Church Head Start location.

Dr. James M. Lawson was the pastor of the church, a leader of the nonviolent movement and a teacher of Dr. King. Nonviolence was at the heart of how the school operated.

My father retired from the U.S. Post Office, as did many of my father's family. My father was a leader in high school, the military, the post office and the community. He was a union representative in the post office in the late 1960s, '70s and early '80s. He orchestrated one of the first work stoppages of the federal government.

Both parents instilled in my brother and me that leaders must be above reproach to demand rights and be voices for the masses. We were taught that fear should not stop us from moving. We were shown how our names could travel further than our physical bodies and how to make sure our names were honorable.

What has changed? Now we live in a world of isolation. Even though it seems so much easier to be connected, the false sense of connection is what keeps people to themselves. Everyone has some sort of electronic device that keeps them occupied. We don't have to engage with people unless we sincerely want to or are forced to. What was so easy before the '80s must now be taught. Engagement has become an art. Understanding when and how to interact with people is not a common task. It's easier for us to remain in our isolated world because we don't have to be hurt, let down or be misunderstood by people. But to achieve greatness of our best selves, we must engage others.

We learned and grew up in a time when we were forced to interact. Now, so many of us choose to be in our own world. The youth don't have a choice. We must teach them through sharing our lives and having conversations with them. I'm writing this book to remind adults of their childhood and to reignite the engagement beast within them. This is not designed to teach you anything new, but to remind you of how to engage our youth.

THE JOURNEY

WE WILL BE TRAVELING ON THIS JOURNEY through the lens of five young adults called Students 1–5, 20 male teenagers called focus group A and myself, both as a youth and with my adult experiences while working in school systems. Hopefully, this will give you a broad perspective and you will be able to identify with one of the examples.

Student 1

Student 1 is a 16-year-old black female. Student 1 has moved from her mother's home to her father's home to her grandmother's home and back to her mother's home. Her mother had her at 17 years of age. She left school because she was bullied. She stays isolated and does not have any outside activities, yet she loves to draw.

Student 2

Student 2 is a 16-year-old black male. He has dropped out of school because at school he was always being told that the next thing he did would cause him to be kicked out. He admits that he did get in trouble and spent some time at the alternative school, but he was looking forward to a second chance. He felt that his zoned school was trying to get him removed from their system. At first, his mother did not want to take him out, but when she met with the school administrators and saw what they were trying to do, she withdrew him.

Student 3

Student 3 is an 18-year-old black male. He attended high school but became disinterested when they stopped offering Pathways, a school program that aligns course work and classes with a particular career. Currently he is working on his high school equivalency diploma. His mother takes him to school and picks him up every day.

Student 4

Student 4 is a 20-year-old black male. Before studying for his high school equivalency diploma, he received a letter stating that he could not return to his zoned school. He did not have a clue why and his mother did not take him back to his zoned school to get him back in.

Student 5

Student 5 is a 17-year black male who lives in a foster home. His mother lives in Florida. He has a lot of challenges on top of being quiet and reserved. He does not trust many people.

Focus Group A

Focus Group A represents 20-plus young teenage males, ages ranging from 11 to 13. There is a mixture of backgrounds, skill, academic, behavioral and economic levels.

STEPS

I.
KNOW THEIR NAME

CALLING SOMEONE BY HIS/HER NAME is one of the highest forms of respect in the black community; especially after fighting the terms associated with black adults such as boy, girl, them or those people. We know that generalizing robs people of their individuality. What about generalizations that show others in a positive light instead of a negative one? Let's do a little exercise. Think about each of the words listed below. Be honest with yourself, what human image comes to mind with each word?

- Powerful
- Smart
- Hard-working
- Native
- Lazy
- Thug

Calling a person by his/her name is one of the first Steps in Engagement. It shows a greater sense of value and respect for them as an individual. Have you ever heard that the sweetest and most important sound to a person is the sound of their own name? Well, it's true. As my work includes engaging students from K-16, an example to illustrate this instantly comes to mind. One day as I walked down the hall of a high school, I noticed one of the school monitors addressing a young man about why he was in the hall.

The monitor didn't know his name and upon questioning him, the student became irritated. The source of the irritation was because the hall monitor was talking at him, not to him. I had known this young man since he was in the fifth grade. I wanted to intervene to prevent what I saw turning into a potentially bad situation for the student. I called the young man's name during the back-and-forth and increasingly hostile interaction. They both came to a complete standstill. The student responded to me, and I asked him to correct his behavior and apologize to the school monitor.

Due to the history of me knowing the student's mother, his neighborhood and most of all, him, there was a positive outcome. I've been in that same scenario before without knowing the students' names and there were totally different outcomes.

Using that same example, you can draw the conclusion that knowing someone's name represents the fact that you at least know something about them. Do you know the individual, their lineage, friends and community or can you relate to their reality? By knowing their name, chances are you have a good idea of one or more of those facets of their background.

CASE STUDY

How do you feel when an adult who you respect or look up to does not know your name?

Student 1:
When someone does not know or remember my name, I feel as if I do not exist. My mother does not even say my name unless she wants me to do something for her. Other times she just says, "Hey you . . ."

Student 2:
The only time anyone at the school remembered my name was when they wanted to write me up, even for things I did not do. I just felt like they wanted me to be removed from the school.

Student 3:
It really does not bother me. It is what it is.

Student 4:
It does not bother me.

Student 5:
It does not bother me because I sometimes do not remember people's names. But if they do remember my name, it makes me feel important.

Group A:
Their answers ranged from doesn't matter, to disrespected, to normal, to weird, to invisible, to feeling like an outsider.

There was a young man who was struggling between the way he was being raised and the life he wanted to live. He didn't have a relationship with his father in his teenage years and he really missed that. He was at a crossroads of who he was and finding his purpose. I became a male role model for him, the father figure that he lacked, as I did for many of the students I worked with during my time in the schools.

He was cast out of the schools as a troublemaker, forced to make his way in the streets. Reputation is everything to someone who doesn't breathe the air of the American Dream. He tried life in the streets, but that was not him. After many talks about who he was and what connects him to something bigger, he started trying to walk another path. It was difficult because of the baggage he carried from his past. This is the case with many students. They ask me, "Why change? They will still see me as I was." Just like I respond to them, I told him that his name is more than what we call someone. It represents who he is, "so fight to maintain what you want your name to represent."

Unlike this young man, my father was my hero. I admired him to the point where, when I was around 5 or 6 years old, I told him and my mother that I wanted to change my name to my father's name. I wanted to be known as Junior. So, from that point on, my father instilled in me what our last name represents. It represents all my relatives who have gone on before, as well

Step I. Know Their Name

as those who will live on after me. There are two things we have in this world: our name and our word. My mother taught my brother and me that people should fight with all they have to protect their name. That gave my brother and me a sense of pride in everything we did because of who we are.

When you know others' names, it gives them a deeper sense of pride. It makes them want to uphold the image of themselves that you have in your head. More than likely, they will want to own up to a positive or more endearing version of the person you know. This is not saying that you have to pretend to be best friends with them. This is suggesting that an interaction that aims to have a hopeful outcome should be driven by a connection stronger than that of complete strangers.

Have you ever acted in a carefree, almost reckless manner because you were in a place where you were sure no one knew you? How about done something and thought, "Oh gosh! These people know who I am!" When you are aware that people know you, the stakes are higher.

The same is true with our youth. The stakes are higher when they are aware you know their name—and you use it! That makes them aware that the interaction taking place will be filed into a memory box of sorts, always associated with them. I don't like to bring up the past, especially with someone who I am trying to reach. They already feel like the world only sees them as the person they were, not who they are trying to be. But, they also know that I have attached every interaction we have had to their name. In this way, using names makes people take ownership.

If you have trouble remembering names, especially if you are dealing with a sizable population, here are a few ways to put forth a good effort.

Focus on them.

You can't learn about a person if you are not paying attention to them. When making their acquaintance, also make eye contact and give them a firm handshake. Ask their name, then use it immediately, "Hi, Chase, nice to meet you."

Ask a question.

In the urban community, it's common to hear names that are unique and possibly difficult to pronounce. They want to know that you care enough not to butcher it. Ask a question about where they are from or where you are meeting them. "Derrion, how long have you been living on this side of town?" Give them the opportunity to correct your pronunciation while showing some level of genuine concern.

Use image association.

Remembering names is a tricky science. If you know someone else who has that name, picture them when speaking to the new person as a point of reference. Name alliteration works for some, where you think of a characteristic that matches their personality, like Friendly Fred. Or use imagery from a part of your conversation. If Fred tells you his passion is football, picture him tossing a football. Different images work for different people. Find what works best for you.

In business, calling someone by his/her name indicates personal feelings for that person. It shows a level of respect and whether or not you like them. Why? Because when you like someone, you pay more attention to them. In a way, it becomes their brand. That is what we want our youth to realize. They are a brand. Their actions and behaviors speak volumes about who they are as a person—their personal brand. We want to encourage them to be stand-up individuals who contribute positively to society through their personal brand.

SELF-REFLECTION

How important is your name in your life?

How important is a person's name as it relates to their individual identity?

Name a time where someone did not remember your name. How did it make you feel?

Write down three ways to help you remember names.

~ Notes ~

II.
LISTEN

THIS IS ONE WORD that has been given several definitions. One of the definitions more appropriately belongs to the words hear or hearing. Listening deals with being actively engaged in what others are saying so much that one connects with the individual's core through their emotions.

Many times, my taking the time to listen to a student prevented a fight or verbal altercation that could have had a violent end. I'm fortunate that many fights didn't happen around me in my 20 years of working in schools. Many would say it's because of my size; I stand 6 foot 4 inches. However, I know a few men even larger than I am who would quickly say that has not been the case for them. I give listening all the credit. I hear what the students are saying directly and indirectly, by words, body language, facial expressions and actions.

There was one young man in middle school who found himself in trouble quite often. He loved his mother, but being raised without a father or a positive male influence in his life had him reaching out for that connection. As many of our young men do, he turned toward peers who led a life in the streets. I knew he really didn't want that kind of life, but in his desperation he started selling crack on a corner.

I got wind of him skipping school and standing on the corner instead of being in school. Because he had made me aware of his aspirations and what he wanted out of life, I jumped in my car during the middle of the school day to get him off that corner. I was told I was crazy for putting any effort into him but I knew his desires and his true character because I had listened to understand him. As soon as I pulled up, I stepped out of the car and told him to get in. At first he hesitated, then he got in. I took him back to school and he stayed with me the rest of that day. Had I known that he really wanted that type of life, I would not have gone to get him. There would have been a different approach in my attempt to reach him.

Listening is key to connecting with someone even if we don't see them as our equals, especially with our youth. My senior year in high school, I was one of the top football players in Memphis. My goal was to be known as the top athlete. I expressed this to my mother and father as we discussed how to approach my last year in high school as far as the media and extra attention that would be thrust upon me. My mother listened to what I wanted. As we talked, she suggested that under no circumstance should I commit to a school until after track season. My father and I agreed. But the press coverage, plus the excitement and hype around the first signing day caused me to forget about my goal. I got caught up in the glimmer and glitz of National Signing Day and announced my decision.

During track season, I won the state track meet in the 110-meter high hurdles, third place in the high jump and set the state record in the decathlon. That event, on top of my football success, signified that I was the best athlete in my city, being a blue-chip football player and an All-American in track. If I had waited until track season, more schools would have offered me scholarships. I still learned a huge lesson after reflecting on that experience: the minute of fame can take you far off your course. Slowing down and listening can be one's best guide.

I developed a genuine appreciation for my mother listening to me. Unlike many other adults, my mother realized that her purpose was not in the moment, but to lay a foundation for my future. Going forward, her words had more weight because of that situation. Not only did she prove that she was truly listening then, she did it over and over again.

As adults, we must remember that we are to plant seeds in the lives of our youth though we will not always see their growth.

CASE STUDY

How do you feel when adults don't listen to you?

Student 1
I do not talk to my mom because she never listens. She asks me a question, then answers it herself, never taking the time to listen to what I have to say. I stay to myself.

Student 2
I can talk with my mom. Other than her, I really do not talk with other adults. If I tried to talk with someone and they were not listening, I would not speak to them again.

Student 3
I feel disrespected.

Student 4
It upsets me. The first time they try to say that they do not understand me, I will try to talk with them again, and if they react the same way, I will never go to them again.

Student 5
It bothers me; however, what really makes me mad is if someone who does not know me tries to tell me what to do without listening to me about the situation. I can sometimes get so mad that I am ready to fight.

Group A

Several of the young men said they feel disrespected and ignored. A couple of the young men said they feel like a joke. The most eye-opening answer was one young man who said it makes him feel like a ghost. That was the first time I had ever heard that response.

Throughout my tenure in a school dedicated to working with the most challenging student behaviors, I learned the difference in hearing versus listening. At the beginning of spring every year, a local carnival comes to a certain part of the city. I guess you can say it's the event that kicks off spring. The school I am referring to has students who were kicked out or administratively placed in one location from all over the city. Yes, it is one of those ideas that look great on paper. Few schools would welcome this magnitude of challenge due to the presence of students from every neighborhood and every public housing community. Needless to say, we were in for a very, very hard three weeks of schooling during the time of the spring carnival.

During the carnival, any beef or altercation would be amplified to the 10th power. Imagine altercations between teens that had ended only to resurface when they became classmates or saw each other in school.

It was my first spring in Atlanta. While working at an alternative school we had double-digit fights on a Monday. It was the first week of the spring carnival. We thought it was just neighborhood challenges spilling over into the school. The same thing occurred on Tuesday, so I was starting to get concerned because the students lived in totally different neighborhoods from the altercations that happened on Monday. I housed the students in my office until parents were contacted. I kept all the students who were on one side of an altercation together, so I could do what we call "ear hustling" or eavesdropping. I seemed to be busy on the computer so the students would think I was preoccupied.

Tuesday raised my concern because a few female and male students who don't normally get into confrontations were involved in a big fight. I knew it was not those students' normal behavior. I had the opposing students, the ones who seemed to be the usual aggressors, in my office. As the students were in my office, one student stated that she was not the girl they were after. The other student said she was with the one that started it so they settled on fighting her. Then I asked them some questions. These young ladies did not say much, but I expected that to happen.

I switched groups and brought in the young ladies who I had a bond with and asked them a couple of questions. They hesitated opening up at first. Then I asked one young lady why did the other young ladies think she was with the group they were going to fight at the carnival. She was shocked that I had that information. She explained what happened, which prompted the others to want to give their side. The whole story initiated at the carnival.

Not being an Atlanta native, I didn't have a true understanding of how the carnival would influence the challenges we faced during those weeks. By Wednesday, it was the same thing, only different students. I was so bewildered. I was used to dealing with and de-escalating all types of gang and neighborhood wars. This was not that.

As the week progressed, I knew extra measures had to be taken. On Thursday, I talked with a few different students who had influence in the school and their neighborhoods. I asked them, "What in the world is going on?" They told me that the carnival was the place where everything started. Other than our school, it was the only place where students from all over the city gathered. When incidents happened at the carnival, the aftermath would spill over to school once the kids saw each other again.

To be proactive, I asked them what could I do to stop this from happening. They gave me some good ideas. I listened. To my surprise, they told me that if the staff and I would listen, students would talk about what was going to happen before a fight started.

You see, the art of listening is more than the physical act. Most people listen just so they can respond. Listening is to understand what people say so you can process it. Effective listening also demonstrates how strong a leader you are. The increasing popularity of social media has given everybody a voice. Knowing how frequently our youth interact on social media shows that they want to be heard. Take advantage of what they have to say.

Listening is such a valuable skill that you really get to learn a lot about the youth. You also gain their respect by taking the time to interact with them, which is priceless. It helps you manage their mood, their productivity and perhaps most importantly, their interaction with other youth.

Step up your listening skills:

- ➢ Take the time to interpret what you hear.
- ➢ Don't be afraid to ask for clarity if necessary.
- ➢ Ask open-ended questions.
- ➢ Minimize your shock about their answers.

In my experience, listening to the kids around me helped to dissipate some potentially hostile situations. How could listening benefit you?

SELF-REFLECTION

What are some characteristics of a good listener?

After the reading the chapter, how can I use what I have learned to improve my listening skills with youth?

Name a situation where you were not listening. What were the consequences of not listening?

What are some things that I can say to let the person know that I am listening?

~ Notes ~

III.
DON'T JUDGE

JUDGMENT IS USED SO LOOSELY. It seems that we only use it when it benefits us. We are quick to say, "Don't judge me," yet we judge others. In this section, not passing judgment means allowing someone to be themselves and express themselves freely without the other individual expressing preconceived notions of how they should act, dress, speak and worship.

My first week as a graduation coach in a middle school, I was called to the counselor's office over the intercom. Before I could leave my office, I was met at my door by the principal who said I was needed in the counselor's office. With this type of attention, I was wondering, "What am I walking into?"

As I walked into the counselor's office, I saw a group of people: a mother and daughter, the principal, assistant principal, counselor and the behavior coach. The mother was stating that she didn't trust any of us because no one tried to help her daughter when she was previously at this school. The principal introduced me to the mother and her daughter, then told them

I would be her point of contact since her daughter would be a part of my caseload. The principal stated that I was new to the school and this would give her daughter a fresh start. We went to my office and talked for more than an hour, coming to an agreement that we would work together for the best interest of her daughter.

This was a perfect strategy the principal devised. The young lady had cursed out everyone in that room on more than one occasion. Allowing me to work with her was placing her in a judgment-free zone. I didn't know them or what had happened in the past before meeting them. It was because of not having that judgment that our bond became as strong as that of a father and daughter. Ten years have passed since she was in the seventh grade and to this day, this former student calls me father and keeps me updated with what is happening in her life.

She was interviewed by a close friend and asked about our relationship:

> I have known Mr. Carpenter since the seventh grade. He has had such an impact in my life. Whenever I call him, he always has time for me. He has and still is encouraging me. He has taught me to never give up. There have been quite a few times when I wanted to give up and he would not let me. He tells me I can do it. An example is with high school. I thought that I had done everything to get my high school diploma and I found out that I needed another credit. I just gave up. Mr. Carpenter kept telling me the importance of getting my diploma even if I

Step III. Don't Judge

> go get my GED because I will need it to enter either college or start a career. He never lets me give up. He is someone who I can always talk to without being judged. He listens and if he doesn't know an answer to a question, he finds out the information. Not too many adults will do that. He is more than a teacher and mentor; he is the father that I need. He inspires me to be the best version of myself.

When someone knows they can speak to you without judgment, it opens the lines of communication. Even if they are somewhat hesitant to talk to you initially, once they know they can trust you that is just what they will do. They become authentic and vulnerable; they will share with you what they want and need. It is up to you to be appreciative of that space. Realize that you are being held in high esteem if they trust that they can talk to you without being judged.

In my personal life, I was attending a training session in California on nonviolent communication. In an environment that was supposed to be filled with people who were there to spread the teachings of nonviolent communication to end oppression, there were people who were still practicing oppression subconsciously. During one session that centered on race, I shared that even as a 50-year-old man I am still seen in the eyes of many as someone who is not educated or not on their level—until they hear that I work with Emory University. Then some of those same people instantly change their opinion of me.

***

As the session continued, a few people started crying due to the testimonies in the circle. One woman said that she knows now that she has to change herself and apologized to me. This gave me pause, not knowing what she was referring to. She said I had (correctly) described her as one of the people who looked down on me. Even though upon introduction we stated where we worked, in her mind it never clicked. Once we were in the same small group for a session and she realized that I worked for a certain university, only then her views of me changed. This change was due to where I worked, not for who I am. It did not have anything to do with my speech, how polite I was or what issues I had overcome in my past. She judged me solely based on skin color.

As a young man, I had mostly been put into a certain category based on my looks rather than on knowing who I am. I am a dark-skinned black man who stands 6 foot 4 inches and has had a gold tooth for the majority of my life. Many people assume I grew up in the hood and have approached me in that way. My mother has three degrees and worked as an educator in the public school system. My father had his bachelor's degree, was an Air Force veteran and worked in management at the U.S. Post Office. My gold tooth came in the summer of 1979 when I broke part of my front tooth. I was about to get a cap so I asked if I could get a gold tooth because my father had one. I had a gold tooth before the drug scene (crack cocaine) came to be as big as it was in the late 1980s and early '90s. We lived in the suburbs of Memphis and I went to a predominantly white middle and high school.

So, in what category would you place a tall, dark-skinned black man with a gold tooth?

Step III. Don't Judge

Would you be able to approach people without bias? Would you be able to hold a conversation with someone without letting your preconceived notions affect your interaction with them? If not, you certainly must try, especially when dealing with our youth. Just like a dog can smell fear, they can sense that you are not looking at them fairly. This will cause them to act out even more. They will shut down and give you the behavior you expect from them.

You do not want anyone judging you; don't make the mistake of doing it to others.

SELF-REFLECTION

Think about a situation in which you were judging someone instead of trying to understand their point of view.

What was the behavior that you objected to?

What were you thinking or what was your response to the behavior?

Put yourself in their shoes; what could have caused that behavior?

How could you have responded differently that would have been more effective?

~ Notes ~

IV.
STAY IN YOUR LANE

THIS IS ONE OF the most important rules that will help you engage youth. In simple terms: Don't impose. This unspoken code is very easy to violate because many times, adults view youth as subservient. This is evident in our daily interactions with them. They are living their lives and we must have permission to enter their space. Even if we have permission to enter their space in one capacity, it doesn't mean we can switch our role whenever we choose while in their space, unless we are granted permission.

One day, I was meeting with a group of middle school students. A couple of them had gotten into some minor trouble. As I was allowing them to fully express themselves about the situation at hand, one student said something that all the students agreed with. They felt that some of the teachers were so concerned with being cool with students that they'd forgotten their role. The teachers tried to become their friends, talking and carrying themselves on the same level as students. I personally knew the teachers they were referring to. I could not change how the students interpreted the teachers' actions.

One of the students was having relationship problems and the teacher noticed something bothering the student. As the teacher questioned the student to help him/her figure out what the issue was, the teacher began to give advice from a friend's point of view rather than that of a caring adult. This robbed the student of the critical thinking process, as well as learning about themselves through overcoming trials. It was interesting listening to the students say things like: Just because we like you as a teacher doesn't make you a friend in our age group, or just because we like you as a mentor doesn't make you our parent.

This brought back some memories of my sixth-grade year. I went to the same school where my mother taught. A couple of girls were talking in the class, so the teacher said be quiet. A few minutes later they started passing notes. The note fell close to my desk. My classmate asked me to hand it to her. I reached down and handed her the note. As usual the teacher saw the latter action, which was me handing the girl the note. The teacher began raising her voice about talking in class, referring to the girl and me.

I hadn't said a word or been in conversation with the girls, but because the teacher had a friendly relationship with my mother, she wanted to use this time to make an example at my expense. I refused to say anything back to her because I didn't want to disrespect her. I guess because I was ignoring her, she said out loud in the class, "I'm going to go tell your mother at lunch." Some of the students said, "Oooh weee!" That made me mad, but I didn't say anything again. Then she repeated it, to which I replied loudly, "Go tell her." She looked stunned

Step IV. Stay In Your Lane

and embarrassed. Just because she worked with my mother didn't give her the right to step outside her professional role.

As adults, we wear many hats. But let's make sure that we only put on the right hat at the right time.

SELF-REFLECTION

What does it mean to stay in your lane?

Think about a time when someone gave you unsolicited advice. How did you feel?

What does it mean to respect boundaries?

What boundaries do you have for yourself that you want others to respect?

How do you establish boundaries, especially interacting with young people?

~ Notes ~

V.
BE PERSONABLE

WE LIVE IN A SELFISH, self-centered world where rules only apply to the individual who has the capacity to and capability of enforcing them. We too often want the rules to apply only when it benefits our cause, purpose and existence; however, when the rule differs from what we want, we sometimes want to bend the rule or forget there even is one.

"Be Personable" falls in this category. To me, being personable is an art. It shows others that you are relatable. In exercising self-improvement, we often forget to work on the way we treat others. Rushing to be a better "us" is not always about our own ambitions but listening to and helping others on their quest to be understood or be better individuals as well.

In my first years working in education, I never understood why students shared things with me that they would not share with anyone else. Then I realized it was because of my work space. It was important for my office to express who I am and what I represented. I played football in college, so I had my college football helmet sitting on the bookcase. Pictures of my children were framed and sitting on my desk. Famous quotes and pictures were framed and hanging on the walls.

I strategically asked that my office be close to the cafeteria so I could have time to host individual and small group sessions during lunch so not to disrupt classroom instruction or take away the student's instructional seat time. We had three lunch periods each day. My office became the place to talk and relax, or as we call it today, a safe space.

One day out of curiosity, I asked a student why he/she liked to come to my office rather than go to the cafeteria. The student said everyone felt safe there, like they were a part of my family because I shared my family life with them. Then it dawned on me, I was able to get personal information because I gave personal information to them.

Now, don't get me wrong. I'm not saying go tell all your business. But ask yourself this question: Would you give someone personal information about yourself if you knew nothing about the individual asking for the information? If I were a betting man, I would bet your answer was, "No."

This brought me back to thinking about the teachers in my past who I had great relationships with. All of them offered a peek into their personal lives, such as whether they were married or not, if they had children, which college they attended and what types of extracurricular activities they participated in during college. I was not doing anything new but what had been done by my teachers all my life.

If you want to connect with teens, you have to give them something to cling to. They have to feel like they are looking

Step V. Be Personable

into parts of your life. Be strategic. If there is something in particular you want to know about them, after the general "hello" and "how are you," talk about aspects of your own life that center around that subject. Knowing that you have had to endure and/or are familiar with some of the obstacles that are front and center in their lives will make them feel like you understand them and where they come from. There's nothing worse than trying to explain something to a person who has absolutely no idea where you are coming from. It will surely cause them to clam up, and well, that defeats the purpose of being personable.

Even with the best of intentions, showing that you care can easily be misconstrued as you just being nosy. Be careful how you come across. Don't use a machine-gun approach when asking questions. That means don't ask question after question after question. Allow for dialogue and even a bit of comic relief in between questions. This further helps to bring down the guard that may be up initially.

SELF-REFLECTION

What is the difference between being personable and personal?

Do you think you make people feel comfortable when they are around you? If so, how?

Step V. Be Personable

If not, what are some things you can do differently?

Write down 10 things that exceptionally personable people do differently than other people.

What are some key things I can do to become more approachable to young people?

~ Notes ~

VI.
POSITIVE SPEECH

We live in a very violent society. Not only because of what we do, but because our thoughts turn into words which turn into actions. Today everyone thinks their opinions are facts, which are shown through social media and even the news. We perceive the person who is first to know something as being more important than the one who actually has the correct information. If you're first, it's almost like a prize: Your thoughts and ideas are held in higher esteem. You impress your feelings on everyone's mind rather than what's correct, relevant and kind. Sarcasm falls into this category as well: using words that signify the opposite of what you really are trying to say, especially in order to insult someone, to show irritation or to be funny. I saw a piece on TV where Ted Koppel was interviewing Sean Hannity. Ted said something that was very profound. Ted said, "It's dangerous when one's ideology is more important than fact."

Negative speech is a form of violence. Many do not consider this a form of violence. We like to think only physical actions are violent. We forget to include subtle, soft-spoken innuendos or even jokes as violent. In some ways, two categories have been created. One is real violence and the other is mean-spirited intention. I ask you, what is the difference? What is the difference in the outcomes of both in the same situation?

Negative voice and sarcasm are widely used by those in power to throw jabs at those in subordinate roles. Parents, teachers, spouses, loved ones and older siblings are some of the biggest perpetrators of negative voice or sarcasm.

"Your daddy ain't nothing," they say, then later, "You're just like your daddy," denoting negative characteristics associated with the daddy or family. Those are just a few examples of mean-spirited language. We are so focused on physical actions as a contributing part of trauma because they are visible proof that someone has been hurt. Many times, we forget words cut, sting, cripple and paralyze people from achieving greatness. Wounds and bruises from physical assaults heal and go away. In time, you may forget they even happened. What will forever be etched in your mind is how someone made you feel, especially during times when you are already being hard on yourself. Others downing us only compound the frustration and hurt we feel.

This is so important because those who hurt us the most with words are those who are closest to us; those we love, revere and admire. The words of strangers don't bother us as much because they don't know us and many times we don't care at all what they think of us. Those we are connected to from the heart are the ones whose opinions matter. So negative speech from someone we allow so close to our hearts and souls can truly have a detrimental effect.

Two statements that have lasting implications are: "You ain't going to be nothing," or "You are stupid." Even though as adults we might be really saying, "If you don't do better you will be on the streets, in jail or dead," the youth hear it the exact way it was said.

CASE STUDY

Have you been told by someone you love, admired or looked up to that you would not amount to anything or you ain't nothing?

Student 1
I have always been told that I would be nothing, I am lazy, too fat and not pretty. In fact, my mom blames me for her getting pregnant at 17 and not being able to keep a boyfriend.

Student 2
When I went to Metro, a juvenile facility, all I heard was, "You ain't never gonna be nothing. Why are you in a hurry to get out, you will be right back in. You guys are dumb and you will never make it in school." I think the system does not want black boys to make it. They want to see us in jail.

Student 3
No, my mom makes sure that I have positive people around.

Student 4
Yes, I have had family members say that I wouldn't be anything. I did not have any support from my parents when I was younger. I wanted it, and to this day I do not understand why I did not get it. I think if I had the support, I would have finished school. I know now that it is up to only me to make something of myself to prove people wrong.

Student 5
When I was little, I was told that I would never make anything of myself. I got into trouble a lot. Then when my mother put me in a foster home, I felt I was not good enough. When your mom doesn't want you, you feel hopeless.

Group A

This question was a very eye-opening experience. Half the room raised their hands when asked this question, indicating that someone was a family member. When I asked them how many have been told that from someone in a school structure, the entire group raised their hands and nodded their heads. I asked what grade were they told that. Half the room said they were told that when they were in the third grade. The third grade is when school starts transitioning from fun to serious. It is the transition from learning to read to reading to learn. It has been stated that this is the grade when boys' reading scores are used to forecast the future prison bed counts. The other young men's answers ranged from first grade to fifth grade. I don't want to put down our teachers, but we have to be careful how we address and talk to our students. We have more power and influence than we realize.

When I was told that I could not achieve something as a child, I was more determined to achieve it and with flying colors. During my ninth-grade year, several high schools courted me to get me to attend their school. I wanted to make my own mark. I was told, "Wooddale High will never be anything," "That white school will not help you with scholarships," and "No one will see you." But, because I had a strong mother and father who instilled in me that cream (greatness) will always rise to the top, I knew I had something to prove.

I chose to go to Wooddale High. At my graduation, they read more than 30 scholarship offers for me from Division 1 and 2 schools. I had positive people in my life from home, my neighborhood and school rooting for me. They were my community. I was one of the lucky ones. Even though there were naysayers in my life, I still had positive influences who let me know that they had my back and encouraged me to be the cream of the crop.

Sadly, I've heard so many adults say to students, "You ain't gonna be nothing." You and I both know that words have power. What do you think happens to those students who hear negative statements like that repeatedly? They begin to believe it. You reading this already shows that you know the power of your impact on our future generations. It also shows how serious you are about your commitment to help them create a brighter future for themselves.

Without a strong community or support system, the statement "You ain't gonna be nothing" can be the main imprint in that child's mind, laying the foundation for a downward spiral. Don't let your words be the trigger of negative thought. Be a rock in support of them. Show that you believe in them and watch how much it means to students not to disappoint you.

SELF-REFLECTION

Are you a positive or negative thinker?

What is the meaning of staying positive?

Why are positive thoughts so powerful?

Name several ways to stay positive—no matter what is going on in your life.

~ Notes ~

VII.
TONE

AS WE UNDERSTAND IT, tone means the pitch and emotion expressed in one's voice. This is something we think is simple, but as time has progressed, maybe it has taken on a deeper meaning or had a different context added to it. This is something we should think about.

The *way* a person voices his/her opinion or concern is what's most important; the delivery. One person can say something one way and it results in a fight; whereas the exact same thing said in a different manner may be received as advice or constructive criticism. The delivery determines how it is received, whether acceptable or disrespectful.

Over the last 15 years or so, people have interpreted looks as having tone. Eyes have always been windows to the soul, meaning you can tell how someone interprets your words by the look on their face and/or in their eyes. Similarly, you can also tell what they may be thinking. However, in recent times, people seem to be more vocal about the way people look at them. The tone in a conversation can easily translate to text messages, social media posts and emails. Simply reading someone else's words can easily yield an unfortunate miscommunication. Just for a moment, let us create our own definition of tone to be the way one expresses emotion through communication.

Many of the coaches with whom I have worked were caring people, even with those who were not athletes. I added the tidbit about athletes because we all know there are preconceived thoughts that athletes are favored in the school and mainly by coaches. My eighth-grade year was a rough one. It was the year I was going through my awkward period. I could not chew bubble gum and walk at the same time. One day, my father had me in the backyard doing drills. No matter how hard I tried, I could not backpedal without falling. I wanted to play basketball on my junior high school team. I tried out and got cut quickly. Probably after my first layup attempt.

My school had a B Team and I was cut from that as well. Coach Duke, who was the B & C teams' coach, could see how badly I wanted to play. He allowed me to ride the bench on the C Team. When I say allowed, he really was doing me a huge favor. I was not good due to my awkwardness; I did not have good height, quickness or any kind of physical potential. What I did have was a drive to play. His tone in talking to me about all the reasons why he should have let me go versus why he kept me on the team helped me see what I could become in life.

I knew a male student who could never escape the positively remarkable history of his older brother. The older brother was an exceptional athlete, but the streets got ahold of him. The younger brother was an exceptional athlete as well. However, he liked school. He would come to my office every morning to speak and sit even if it was just for two minutes before he went to homeroom, and he would put on my college football helmet. During his seventh-grade year I was not in the school and he began to get in a little trouble. From then on, the murmurs about his brother started ringing even louder. Later the streets got him too. The tone of the school and streets dictated his expectations for himself, which were low. He was lost to the streets and soon after to prison for murder at a very young age.

Tone can be encouraging or just the opposite. When talking to the youth, it is good to always remember that, even if you are telling them something that can be good for them to turn their lives around. If your delivery is harsh, it seems like your direction is coming from a hurtful place. Your words will not do any good falling on dry soil. If the child you are trying to reach is offended by your tone, you will be able to tell by his/her responses physically and/or verbally. Once you realize that your words are being taken the wrong way, take a step back, re-evaluate and quickly use a softer or different approach. The last thing you want is for a student to feel attacked.

SELF-REFLECTION

Think back on a situation where someone's tone changed the conversation you were having. How did it make you feel?

How could a change of tone have resulted in a different outcome?

Step VII. Tone

Why is it important to use the right tone of voice, especially when speaking to young people?

Try this: Record yourself and listen to the tone of your voice. Does it match what you are trying to say or is it telling a different story?

~ Notes ~

VIII.
RELEVANCE

Relevance is the connector of multiple factions, be it personal, situational or spiritual. How does one matter or connect to the now? Think about phones that are hooked into the wall. Sure, they were all the rage 40 to 50 years ago. Today? They are few and far between. Why have a phone connected to a wall when you can have a cellphone small enough to fit in your pocket to go wherever you go and has cool functions such as texting and email capacity plus apps? What's the point? Don't be a wall phone when you can be a cellphone. Be relevant.

As adults, we are continuously searching for usefulness and the ability to connect, yet we don't think that our young people are in search of this as well. While co-facilitating a workshop on "Establishing a Beloved Classroom," one of the facilitators made a powerful statement to start the paradigm shift. "Teachers are people who teach and students are people who learn." Overall, the focus is on people not titles. The one relevant factor in this equation is people. In engaging youth, remember they are people, human beings with interests, fears, loves, likes and dislikes. We can not connect to youth when we forget they are human beings.

My trainings and workshops are successful because I take myself out of the main focus. What is the outcome of the workshop and how do I make a connection with the students? How do I tie the information I'm teaching to their lives, environment and culture? Most of the time, I have mini pre-sessions with students around the age of the workshop participants before the workshops begin. This gives me a preview of what to expect and how to make the information more relevant. They will guide me on what's lame, dull, outdated and not relevant.

Since my focus is on enhancing the experience for the students, what they say goes. If my biggest joy is the recognition I would get then I need to get out of this field. The biggest joy should be getting positive feedback on what the young people got out of the session. Was it worth their time? Did it have a positive impact on them and did it help them to move their needle?

One school year, 9/11 fell on the first day at a new school. The school gave me that day to set up my room and get everything ready for my first day with the students. Watching the horrible events made me realize that we are living in a different time and the same old mindset can't be the leader of our creativity today. From that day forward, my mission was to be inclusive of thoughts, ideas and outcomes with my students. This would be easier for me because of the type of school and the class that I taught. I taught a trade, commercial painting and life skills/soft skills in an all-boys detention center. This was a gift:

The detention center job brought me insights I applied to later jobs. I went from working with those who were kicked out of school for breaking laws to working with students who broke school rules. Now I carry the same mindset to the alternative and public schools that I work in.

During lunchtime in the public schools, when the students would hang in my office to have their own space, I would ear hustle—listening without being seen or heard. I noticed that the students had great ideas about how students were being punished in school. They were honest about how adults handled the situations. They even knew when the adult didn't have all the information to make a proper judgment. Due to those conversations, all the activities and programs that I put into place in schools offered a leadership component. That allowed the students to have a voice to build upon for youth empowerment, thus allowing the students to connect their previous experiences and knowledge to the situation at hand. Through this partnership with the youth I would make assignments, workshops and conversations relevant to the students.

An example is a middle school where I was part of a team that created a peer mediation panel for students. The students used restorative practices to change their school culture by focusing on attendance and behavior. That allowed students to empower one student at a time.

We wanted to keep students in school and not suspended. So we trained students to be the leaders in addressing the attendance and behavior challenges in their school.

***

The eighth-grade student team met with a young man who was referred to the peer leaders for classroom disruption in math class. The team members introduced themselves, stated the program's mission and asked him what happened to cause him to be in front of them that day. This was his opportunity to exercise his voice by explaining what happened. After listening to his version, the team then took turns asking their peer questions. One peer leader asked about his plans for the future. He said he wanted to own his own business. Another peer leader asked what type of education and character it took to be an entrepreneur. This made the student stop, connect and reflect. Strategically, one of the members asked how he was doing in math class. He said he was having trouble. Then a peer leader asked where he sat in the class. He said the front. A team member in the same class corrected him, saying, "You sit in the back and play around." He was surprised by the statement yet agreed because this was from a peer, not an adult.

After they finished asking questions, the agreement was made that the student was to verbally apologize to the class and to the instructor, sit in the front of the class and attend tutorials for math. One of the female peer leaders said, "We would like to add one more sanction. We want you to write a letter to yourself. We want you to write about all the good qualities that you have." He agreed but looked surprised. "You must believe in yourself before anyone will believe in you," the peer leader said. "We believe in you and we will be checking on you." His attitude totally changed. He completed all the sanctions. His math grade improved and he started to take on more responsibility and initiative in the school.

SELF-REFLECTION

How comfortable are you personally with relating to young people?

How do you know when you have formed a positive relationship?

After reading the chapter, name three ways you can build a relationship with young people.

~ Notes ~

IX.
BE CONSISTENT

THIS IS THE NEXT TO THE LAST STEP. Many times we do so many things right but because our consistency isn't solid, we are left wondering what went wrong in the relationship. A true test of who we are as an individual can be based on the consistency in our beliefs, core values and standards. Young people don't have as much book knowledge as the average adult; however, they have something that many adults lose due to life and assimilation in this world. It's called mother wit. Young people connect through spirit. The spirit is shown through one's core values, and core values are shown through consistency of actions.

I know that I am a truly blessed man. I've had the great fortune to have had great parents. In this step, I must emphasize the importance of men in the lives of young people. Women have always been in the lives of young people, but I want to talk about modern times where the male presence is limited.

I've had a great and strong father, two grandfathers and seven uncles in my life. I knew I had men teaching me how to lead, be it leading me from the front or recognizing who had my back with support from the rear. From the seventh grade through my senior year in high school, I went to predominantly white schools because we moved from an all-black area in South Memphis to being the third black family in a new neighborhood called Hickory Hill, which was a suburb of Memphis. Within three years, there was an influx of black families to our neighborhood. Even though the Parkway Village, Fox Meadows and Hickory Hill area were mostly white, our small neighborhood had approximately 10 black families in 1978 and more moving in every year. So we still had the village mentality.

All the dads were an extension of our immediate families. I give much praise to Mr. Briggs, Mr. Taylor, Mr. Reddit, Mr. Foster, Mr. Lofton, Mr. Echols, Mr. Hardy and Mr. Walls . . . these were black men who made a difference in my life simply with their consistent presence. Now the flip side to this was going to predominantly white schools; the majority of the men who were consistent role models in my life in the schools were mostly white. I give much praise to Mr. Ray, Coach Duke, Coach Finch, Coach Mangum, Coach W.S. Donald (mentor), Coach Fortner and Coach Gonda. Last but not least are the four black men who had a great influence on me in high school, Coach Ward, Mr. Harris, Mr. Carter and Mr. Gunn.

Why did I emphasize the color of the men? To show you that these steps are real. They break color, economic, nationality and any other barriers that are dividing us as a people. As you can see, I've had a multitude of men who imparted a piece of themselves into my life. I owe the Creator and them to keep the legacy of giving alive and strong.

Step IX. Be Consistent

I've often been asked why I do this type of work. I see that having strong men in my life who were not afraid to show me the way or to lead me is not common. Now I must pay it forward by being the type of man who helped me when I was young.

As a father raising five children, I noticed that most of my children's friends didn't have the active presence of their father. Many of my students didn't have active fathers in their lives. That is where my mission started. Fatherhood is not just caring for your own child, because in today's society our children will be interacting with children without a father's presence. In order to give what I was given as I grew up, I owe it to the great men in my life to be a positive male role model in my community.

My definition of fatherhood is a man who takes on the responsibility of his community, from the land to the people. Fatherhood means not being afraid to talk to, question, challenge, correct and praise those in the community. Fatherhood simply means loving the community.

So many times, when we (older adults) refer to the good old days and mention the village, we talk about whipping as the main form of discipline and being home before the streetlights came on. Instead, I want us to focus on the discipline that allowed engagement to happen before and after the physical violence took place. Back in the day, an adult was always watching. If something didn't seem right they would question us as to what we were doing, what were our names and where did we live. That is, if they didn't know already. We would still try to lie or manipulate the truth, but adults then would seek out our parents to let them know what happened.

Today I hear so many adults say that they are afraid to say something to children because of what either the child or the child's parent might say or do. Children raise and lower to the standards set by adults. If you show fear, the children will utilize and manipulate the situation.

During my time of working in the many types of schools, from detention centers and alternative schools to public schools and charter schools, the one thing that bounces off my skin is someone cursing me out. Quite a few students have cursed me out on our first encounter. Because I was consistent in my job and beliefs as to the work I was doing, those same students became some of the mentees who needed me the most. I am not telling you to take that kind of abuse; rather, understand who you are and why you are doing what you are called to do. We cannot get preoccupied by the battle but must focus on the war. My war is to remove barriers that can hinder the smooth transition of knowledge that will empower one to his/her greatness. This is what the men in my life did for me.

My father, Robert Earl Carpenter, was one who many looked up to because of his demeanor. He was tall with a commanding voice and a presence that demanded respect. It's a gift he was born with. The other men were very different from my father, but none of them tried to be my father. They were making sure that I lived up to the expectations of my father as a man. The men in my life did this in their own way, which is why they were able to be consistent in their approach and actions.

Being consistent means being you. Not trying to be something you are not or represent a falsehood just to seek power and privilege. Remember, earlier I stated children connect through spirit. I've seen adults portray a fake persona and students made their life so hard many left the school or quit teaching. When you do something you love, you can focus more on the war than the daily battles. Being consistent is simply being true to you.

SELF-REFLECTION

What does it mean when a person is consistent?

Why is it important to be consistent, especially working with youth?

Step IX. Be Consistent

Do you agree or disagree that you are treated the way you teach individuals to treat you?

Name three strategies that help you stay consistent.

~ Notes ~

X.
BE PATIENT

THIS WILL BE THE LAST STEP before arriving at a true connection with our youth. There are many more attributes to help one engage youth. This is just a starting point and reminder to us that our youth will be asking themselves, "What did adults do to connect with us?"

As we arrive on the 10th floor with the 10th and final step, visualize this as the main floor in a stairwell. Young people do skip steps to get to the top quickly. We, too, like to see how many steps we can skip in rushing to get to our destination. The same holds true for the steps of engagement. All the steps are important. All have significance in engaging youth, but every situation doesn't call for completing every step each time. This is where the human element kicks in. Any combination of the steps can help to achieve the engagement you seek from a youth. You don't have to be robotic and try to do every step on every youth. Let it come naturally. Believe that the youth was put in your presence because you already have what it takes to engage them, and they need your engagement to move to the next level. The only steps needed are the ones the youth need from you to engage them.

Today data drives most things because we are going more toward a scientific society than the arts society of the past. One of the mistakes we make in using data is that we do not allow the natural or slow process to take place. We start to see students as numbers or test scores and not as humans.

This happens when a student does one thing today and we hold on to that for the rest of that student's existence at our school or every encounter with that student. But haven't we, as adults, messed up on our jobs? We try to correct the problem we cause quickly and hope it will not come back to haunt us. Why do we want to hold on to the old ways of our youth? Can we let go and start over fresh with a new day? I was told, "Want for your brother as you want for yourself."

Through the years, I've learned to treat each student as I would want to be treated and that is to focus on the human element, the child. This is one thing we know that is true: Students need to be educated, therefore students are the focus of my work. I don't approach this from a scientific perspective at all. I am one person who is called on to help connect students to their education either through a program, mentorship or one-to-one engagement because I am patient with the youth. I do have expectations and hold them to it, but I understand that it will not happen overnight. Patience is a major key when engaging our youth.

SELF-REFLECTION

Why is patience important?

I get impatient when . . .
(Fill in the blank, e.g. stuck in traffic, miss a deadline)

I feel . . . when it happens.
(Describe how you feel physically and emotionally)

When . . . happens, what can I do to calm down?
(E.g., describe some techniques that can help)?

~ Notes ~

CLOSING

I WOULD LIKE TO THANK YOU FOR taking this journey with me. It is imperative that adults be the wise leaders for our youth. We must show them the way through our experiences, love and support. This is easy from our frame of reference, but does it match the youth's perspective? Hopefully, this book will marry the two into one cohesive community of love, respect and empowerment.

For the adults, I would like you to walk away with a connection to your past that can be shared with the youth to establish a better sense of compassion and connection to them. This can be done through sharing experiences, understanding what mistakes they may encounter, allowing them to make those mistakes, be there to help pick them up and tell them that it is not the end of the world. We live in a time where self-preservation supersedes the beloved community, which fosters our solo existence. I hope this book will remind us of how we became our greater selves and remind us that just as someone poured his/her love for our greatness into us, we must do the same for our youth. These steps symbolize the following: to lead we must guide. The steps are for us to walk with our youth, not dictate where and how they should walk. Once we walk with our youth, they will follow, take the baton and run with it. Look at all the liberation movements. Adults started them, but involving the youth caused a change to be made.

To change our world, we must change the way we engage and connect with the next generation of leaders. Youth who develop a positive connection with adults are more often invested in their education and community.

Let's live up to our best selves and connect with our youth better than we did yesterday so that we can inspire them to be their best selves today.

ABOUT THE AUTHOR

Bevin Carpenter

Known as the "Guru of Engagement," Bevin has facilitated workshops and programs for students, parents, communities and agencies for more than 15 years. His philosophy is "Train up an individual and they will not depart from it."

Bevin received his bachelor's degree from the University of Memphis and his MBA from Strayer University. He has served on several boards, including the Georgia State Superintendent Dropout Prevention Taskforce, Fulton County Community Restorative Board, Fulton/Atlanta School Justice Pathway and currently is a member of the 2018 Boys and Men of Color Executive Director Collaborative Circle Cohort. Bevin has been a presenter at several conferences. His article, "Empowering Students to Be Change Agents," was published by Youth Today.

You can find him on LinkedIn.

About the Artist

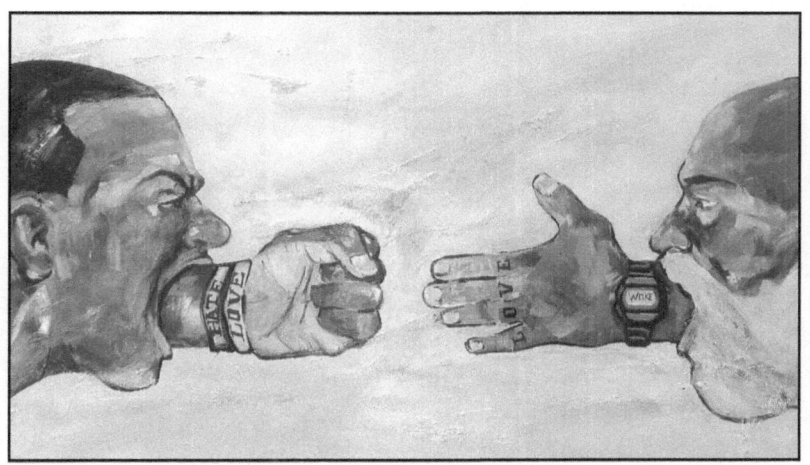

Orin Carpenter

Having a passion to help others find their creative voice, Orin Carpenter works with high school art students to help them etch their mark in society. After receiving his Bachelor of Fine Arts from the University of Memphis, he worked as a graphic designer for several Fortune 500 companies. He continued to work as a graphic designer/illustrator while attending the Academy of Art University, where he received his master's.

His work can be found in the following publications: International Contemporary Artists, Incite 3: The Art of Storytelling, Incite 4: Relax, Restore, and Renew, Professional Artist Magazine and Grace Magazine. Orin's solo exhibitions include: Lost in translation, Incarcerated Souls, Passion is Color, and Metamorphosis.

Visit www.orincarpenter.com to learn more about his passion and his work.

Quotes

Bevin Carpenter's short yet powerful book "Building Bridges" provides a clear path towards authentic youth engagement centered in love. I highly recommend this book to anyone who is willing to do the "heart work" required to realize increased student success in life and the classroom.

> —*Nathaniel Smith*
> *Founder & CEO*
> *Partnership for Southern Equity*
> *Atlanta, Georgia*

Bevin Carpenter's "Building Bridges: 10 Steps to Engage Youth" is such a breath of fresh air in educational writing. Before you finish the first chapter, you can feel Bevin is a man on the ground who truly knows the hearts and minds of the youth. This book is the perfect complement for a professional development retreat or conference where educators can collaborate on ideas of how to take a positive and professional approach in working with young people who we know are thirsting for connection.

> —*Tim Navone*
> *President*
> *Marin Catholic High School*
> *San Francisco, California*

In a world where it seems people are focused more on building walls than bridges, this heartfelt and power packed book on youth engagement is sorely needed. This is a must read for anyone serious about doing meaningful youth development work. Bevin engages the reader with practical, real world examples, and solutions. This is a book that will help you build bridges in every facet of your life!

> —*James Roland*
> *Senior Director*
> *Emory University's Civic &*
> *Community Engagement*

www.ingramcontent.com/pod-product-compliance
Lightning Source LLC
Chambersburg PA
CBHW031425290426
44110CB00011B/524